DINOMUMMY

THE LIFE, DEATH, AND DISCOVERY OF DAKOTA, A DINOSAUR FROM HELL CREEK

DINOMUMMY

THE LIFE, DEATH, AND DISCOVERY OF DAKOTA, A DINOSAUR FROM HELL CREEK

Dr. Phillip Lars Manning

FOREWORD BY TYLER LYSON

KINGFISHER

BOSTON

KINGFISHER

Edited by Hannah Wilson
Designed by Mike Davis
Cover design by Mike Buckley
Picture research by Cee Weston-Baker
Production by Nancy Roberts and Lindsey Scott
DTP by Catherine Hibbert and Nicky Studdart

KINGFISHER
a Houghton Mifflin Company imprint
222 Berkeley Street
Boston, Massachusetts 02116
www.houghtonmifflinbooks.com

First published in 2007
10 9 8 7 6 5 4 3 2 1
1TR/0807/WRLDPRNT/SCHOY(SCHOY)/157MA/C

LIBRARY OF CONGRESS CATALOGING-IN-PUBLICATION DATA
Manning, Phillip Lars, 1967–
   Dinomummy / Dr. Phillip Lars Manning ; foreword by Tyler Lyson.—1st ed.
      p. cm.
   Includes index.
   ISBN-13: 978-0-7534-6047-4
   1. Hadrosauridae—North Dakota—Juvenile literature. 2. Dinosaurs—North Dakota—
Juvenile literature. 3. Mummified animals—North Dakota—Juvenile literature. I. Title.
   QE862.O65M24 2007
   567.914—dc22
                                        2007002878
ISBN 978-0-7534-6047-4

Printed in China

This book is dedicated to anyone who has picked up a fossil and dreamed of lost worlds and forgotten lives.

Dr. Phillip Lars Manning

Contents

Foreword

I have been passionate about dinosaurs ever since my oldest brother, Ryan, and I found the fossilized jaw of a duck-billed hadrosaur when I was six years old. The fossil, which I still have in a shoebox in my bedroom, made me want to learn everything about hadrosaurs and all of the other dinosaurs.

The fossil also made me realize that anyone can hunt for and find dinosaurs. At the age of six, I was too young to look for fossils by myself, but I was very determined. I managed to persuade my very patient and loving mother to drive me out to the remote Hell Creek badlands, which surround my hometown of Marmarth, South Dakota. She would sit in a lawn chair with one eye on her book and one eye on me as I dug around in the dirt, looking for more dinosaur bones.

A large and heavy dinosaur, Dakota moves cautiously on
thick, muscular legs to reach the river's edge. The toes of his
padded feet spread wide to stop him from sinking into the wet
sand, and his tail sways gently to balance his long body. He is not
yet an adult, but already he is almost 26 feet long, nearly the length
of a bus. Dakota drops onto slender forearms, ready to drink.

Suddenly, across the water, two male *Pachycephalosaurus* clash in a violent display of strength. Dakota watches as they charge at each other like battering rams, delivering powerful blows with their thick, domed skulls. Today, their aggressive head butts are designed to impress females of their type. On other days, they might be used in defense against predators.

Another plant eater is quietly watching the contest. The three-horned *Triceratops* is better prepared for defending herself against the giant carnivores of Hell Creek. A heavy and powerful creature, around twice the size of a rhinoceros, she can cause severe damage with her two longest horns while remaining protected by her solid neck frill. Dakota has no such armor or weapons.

13

Dakota returns to the protection of his herd, which is grazing nearby. These gentle plant eaters rely on safety in numbers. Young and vulnerable, Dakota buries himself in the center of the group.

It is the fall, and the hadrosaurs have just arrived in Hell Creek. Every year, they migrate from the north to escape its cool, dry winters. Hell Creek is warm and wet all year round, and the herd has come to feed on its lush plant life.

A lone *Ankylosaurus*, slow and heavy under the weight of her armored plates, joins the hadrosaurs. The movements of the dinosaurs do not go unnoticed. From the cover of nearby vegetation, a pack of *Saurornitholestes* quietly emerges. These vicious raptors are stalking the herd, waiting for the right moment to attack.

The *Saurornitholestes* have chosen their victim.
But this time, it is not Dakota or another
hadrosaur—it is the young *Ankylosaurus*.
The predators, intelligent and fast, circle the
dinosaur and snap at her with razor-sharp teeth.

16

As Dakota turns to flee, he sees one of the raptors leap onto the animal's back and climb up it using its curved claws as hooks. But the desperate attacker will struggle to pierce the armored plating of his prey. Then *Ankylosaurus*, with a heavy blow from his large tail club, knocks aside another *Saurornitholestes* like a bowling pin. The battle will be long and hard. Dakota does not stay around to watch.

17

Later, some of Dakota's herd stop to eat. With strong mouths shaped like ducks' bills, they snap leaves and twigs from bushes and grind the food with their teeth. Others, including Dakota, choose to drink, and, one by one, they drop onto all fours to suck up water. It has rained heavily recently, and the river has burst its banks in places, creating useful watering holes.

All of the hadrosaurs remain alert, constantly listening and watching. Suddenly, Dakota looks up. Something large is crashing through the undergrowth.

And it is coming closer . . .

Tyrannosaurus rex! The herd begins to snort and shriek in terror. As the hadrosaurs struggle to turn and flee, they kick clouds of dust into the hot air. The giant predator surveys the scene slowly, looking for an easy victim. She spots a young adult on the far left of the herd. It's Dakota. Mouth bulging with teeth like steak knives, the tyrannosaur begins to stride through the water . . .

It is the end of the day. As the sun sets over Hell Creek, Dakota lies still and silent. He has not survived. Strangely, there are no signs of injury to his body. If he was killed by the *Tyrannosaurus rex*, why wasn't he torn to pieces? Why wasn't he eaten?

Millions and millions of years will pass before these questions find answers. Dakota's body will lie buried in Hell Creek while Earth's continents collide to form towering mountains, ice ages come and go, and humans take their very first footsteps.

But for now, for the dinosaurs of Hell Creek, *a new destruction is just around the corner . . .*

Hell Creek is deathly silent. It is daytime, but the sky is dark and thick with dust. Ferns, desperate for light, struggle to survive, and in the distance, fires eat through forests of giant redwoods. The corpses of *Triceratops*, *Tyrannosaurus rex*, and herds of hadrosaurs litter the landscape.

What happened here? Years after Dakota died, it is thought that a huge comet from space crashed into Earth. The impact created giant dust clouds and tsunamis, and the planet's life cycles were severely damaged. When the plants began to die, so did the plant-eating dinosaurs. Next to fall were the carnivores, who had nothing left to hunt. Some reptiles survived this mass extinction, along with the mammals and birds, which were smaller. *But the age of the dinosaurs was over.*

Digging for dinosaurs

A young man is walking through the remote, dusty hills of
Hell Creek. Tyler keeps his eyes on the ground, looking
for tiny splinters of bone among the crumbling rocks. He has
hunted for dinosaurs in this way for as long as he can remember.
The afternoon sun is fading, and the straps of his backpack are
beginning to gnaw at his shoulders. It is time for him to go
home—empty-handed. But just as he is about to leave, Tyler
finds something that will begin an incredible adventure
and change his life forever. He finds Dakota.

Something has caught his eye. Tyler kneels down to brush away the stones and dirt that loosely cover it. It's a dinosaur bone! By its shape and size, he knows immediately that it is a vertebra, a tail or back bone. It probably belongs to the tail of a hadrosaur, a duck-billed, plant-eating dinosaur. As he sweeps away more of the soil, he finds another vertebra. Then another. Amazingly, the three "verts" are articulated, which means that they are arranged in the correct order. The bones were not washed away in a river or moved around by a hungry scavenger.

It is getting dark now, and the coyotes are beginning to howl. Tyler works quickly to collect the bones. Only two of them have fully "weathered out," exposed by wind, rain, and snow. Gently, he places the two verts in a sample bag and records the site's location with his GPS receiver. Then, turning on his flashlight, he begins the long walk back to his pickup truck. Besides the third, partly buried vert, he doesn't think that there are any other bones left in the ground.

tailbones in
sample bag

DM.1b.1

3 hadrosaur verts!!

It is many months later, and Tyler has sent me an e-mail. I am Dr. Phil Manning, a paleontologist at the University of Manchester in the U.K. Like Tyler, I have loved dinosaurs since my childhood. It all began when I was five years old. My parents took me to the Natural History Museum in London, and its enormous *Diplodocus* skeleton was the most amazing thing I had ever seen. My first find came several years later when, in my own yard, I found a vertebra from an ichthyosaur, an ancient sea creature.

In his e-mail, Tyler describes his own vertebra discovery in Hell Creek. He went back to the site to dig around the hadrosaur tailbone left in the ground. He discovered that it was connected to the rest of the tail! Then he uncovered something even more incredible, and his e-mail included a photograph of it—dinosaur skin! Bumpy, scaly dinosaur skin!

Tyler had found a dinomummy!

A dinomummy is more than just a fossilized skeleton. It has some fossilized "soft tissue" such as skin and possibly organs, too. No one knows exactly how dinomummies form, as they are very rare. When an animal dies, its flesh normally rots away or is eaten by scavengers before it can fossilize.

Dinomummies are incredibly exciting. They can provide the chance to see what a dinosaur really looks like. Does it have spines on its head, scales down its back, or bite marks on its arm? Tyler is not sure how much of his dinosaur is mummified yet, but I want to help him find out. I book the next flight to North Dakota. I am going to Hell Creek.

After a long, long journey, I arrive in Marmarth, Tyler's hometown. It's great to meet Tyler, but there is no time to waste—we jump into my pickup truck and head out into the badlands.

Around an hour later, there we are, on a hill overlooking Tyler's dig site. This is the ultimate dinosaur territory—the amazing Hell Creek Formation, a series of rock layers hundreds of miles wide and almost one mile deep. This layer is the tomb of the very last dinosaurs that lived on Earth: *Triceratops*, *Pachycephalosaurus*, and one of the greatest predators of all time, *Tyrannosaurus rex*. As Tyler and I look out over this ancient landscape, we try to imagine the vast herds of hadrosaurs that grazed there in prehistoric times.

The body of one of them lies before us now, most of it still buried. The bones found so far are articulated and the fossilized skin is in excellent condition, so Tyler believes that the rest of the dinosaur is there, in the ground. But we will not know for sure until we begin a full excavation. We will need to gather scientists for every stage of the dig: geochemists to study the rocks and soil; paleobotanists to look for ancient plant life; mapping experts to chart the shape of the land; and plenty of volunteers to dig up the rocks. No stone will be left unturned—literally!

A few weeks later, a team of scientists and volunteers gathers at the site. Armed with picks and shovels, we start to dig away the "overburden," the tons and tons of soil around the tailbones. For the moment, we have to leave some rock, called the matrix, around the dinomummy to protect it. So we stop digging when we hit a red-colored layer, as this means that we are getting close to the fossilized skin.

Bit by bit, little by little, a shape begins to appear from the ground—the outline of a dinosaur! Although the matrix still hides a lot of the detail, it looks as if our dinomummy is complete!

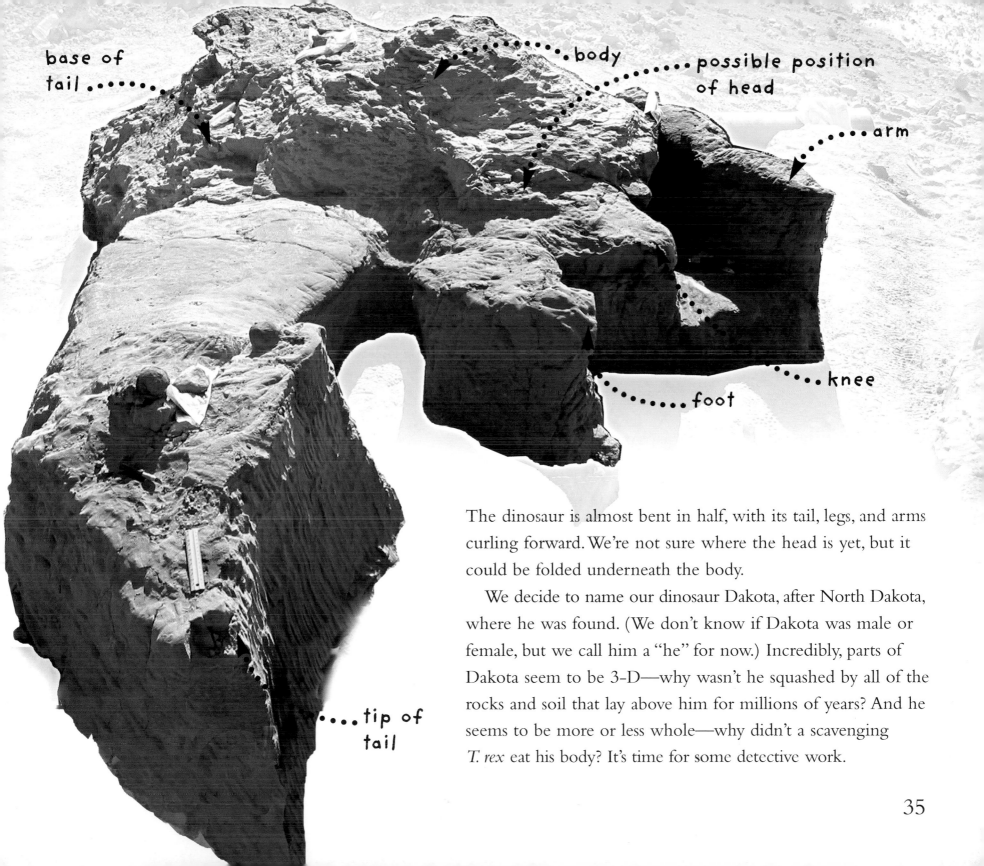

base of
tail

body

possible position
of head

arm

foot

knee

tip of
tail

The dinosaur is almost bent in half, with its tail, legs, and arms curling forward. We're not sure where the head is yet, but it could be folded underneath the body.

We decide to name our dinosaur Dakota, after North Dakota, where he was found. (We don't know if Dakota was male or female, but we call him a "he" for now.) Incredibly, parts of Dakota seem to be 3-D—why wasn't he squashed by all of the rocks and soil that lay above him for millions of years? And he seems to be more or less whole—why didn't a scavenging *T. rex* eat his body? It's time for some detective work.

Dinosaur excavations are all about rocks. Dakota has slowly turned to stone, having fossilized over millions of years, and he is buried in rock. I dig a trench nearby to take a look at the different layers. This area is made up of soft mudstone and sandstone, which might explain why his body was not crushed. I take samples of rock at the same level as Dakota's body and from levels above and below. The rock below Dakota is older than the dinosaur, and the rock above is younger.

Near the bottom of my trench, I notice a strange yellow sulfur ring, which may indicate a decaying plant or animal. As Dakota decayed and fossilized, he also changed the surrounding rock. So, when they are studied later, my rock samples may tell us something about what happened to Dakota.

sulfur ring

rock samples

36

camera

lidar
laser
scanner

On a nearby hill, a "lidar" machine is busily shooting out lasers to different points on the landscape and examining how they bounce back. It uses this information to create a 3-D map. Sitting down with my laptop computer, I take a look at a rough version of the map. Today's rock layers can tell us what the land was like in prehistoric times, and it seems as if Dakota is lying at the edge of an ancient river. Now it is starting to make sense! Perhaps the dinosaur's body was buried quickly in wet sand before a *T. rex* had time to munch it up! And the water from the river probably helped the chemical process that mummified Dakota. But does the river explain how the dinosaur died?

Did Dakota drown?

3-D map

While I discuss dino life and death with Tyler, scientists Professor Rob Gawthorpe and Dr. Kevin Taylor uncover something interesting—cement. Not the cement that holds houses together, but the natural type that holds rocks together. This reddish-brown rock (siderite) encased the dinosaur in a rocky coat of armor, cementing the mudstone and sandstone together. Without it, Dakota would have disintegrated millions of years ago.

Soon afterward, Tyler finds a fossilized leaf. It is the same age as Dakota and the rest of the Hell Creek Formation—65 to 67 million years old. Is the leaf another clue? The leaf belonged to a flowering tree like a modern sycamore. Today, there are no trees, but prehistoric Hell Creek was bursting with lush, green vegetation. When plants rot away, they affect the chemicals in the soil. And it was the chemistry of the ground that preserved Dakota so beautifully. Tyler's leaf is another clue, because, in some small way, it helped turn Dakota into a dinomummy.

sycamore tree

Tyler's fossilized leaf

siderite

After many long, hard days, the dig is over. It is time to pack our bags and leave Hell Creek. There's only one problem—we have to pack an enormous, ten-ton dinosaur, too. To stop moisture from seeping into the matrix, we cover Dakota with tinfoil until he looks like a giant turkey ready for the oven! Then Tyler dips strips of sackcloth into buckets of thick, white plaster of Paris and lays them over the dinomummy. The plaster will set to form a hard, protective covering called a field jacket. Tyler and the team must work quickly because the plaster dries rapidly in the hot sun.

As we cover our mummy in plaster, it gets bigger and bigger and heavier and heavier. No digger will be able to lift it! Luckily, we find a natural break at the base of Dakota's tail. After days of carefully cutting and digging along the break, the tail is gone, leaving two more manageable chunks of dinosaur. Then we drill under the body block so that we can insert a metal support frame beneath it.

Dakota's tail was carefully removed from here.

Finally, both the tail and the body are lying on metal frames, encased in their tough, white field jackets. As Tyler and I wait for the digger to arrive, we look at the enormous three-ton tail block. We are proud of Dakota's tail—it is the first mummified hadrosaur tail ever found. And it looks as if the skin and flesh of the tail extend beyond the last vertebra. This would mean that hadrosaur tails were longer than scientists currently think they were. We will not be able to confirm this until we examine the dinomummy properly, but Tyler and I are sure that *Dakota is going to rewrite hadrosaur history!*

tip of skin?

tip of tailbones

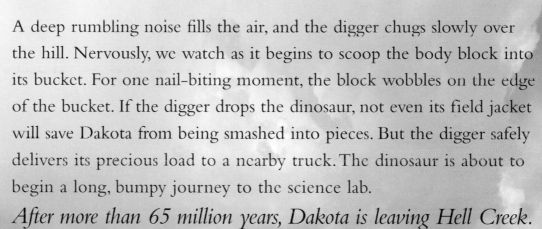

A deep rumbling noise fills the air, and the digger chugs slowly over the hill. Nervously, we watch as it begins to scoop the body block into its bucket. For one nail-biting moment, the block wobbles on the edge of the bucket. If the digger drops the dinosaur, not even its field jacket will save Dakota from being smashed into pieces. But the digger safely delivers its precious load to a nearby truck. The dinosaur is about to begin a long, bumpy journey to the science lab.

After more than 65 million years, Dakota is leaving Hell Creek.

Secrets from the grave

In a dark, dusty laboratory, Dakota has begun to emerge from his rocky armor. Several weeks have passed since the dinosaur bumped and juddered away from the wilderness of Hell Creek to the cool quiet of the lab. When the dinosaur arrived, we began work on the tail block first, cutting away its field jacket with circular saws. Now we pick up smaller tools to begin the "preparation" work. We scrape away the tail's protective rock matrix. As we work, we take more soil samples, wrapping them in plastic and stacking them on the section from which they came. The process is slow and painstaking, but the goal is simple—to remove as much of the encasing rock as possible. We want to leave nothing but dinosaur.

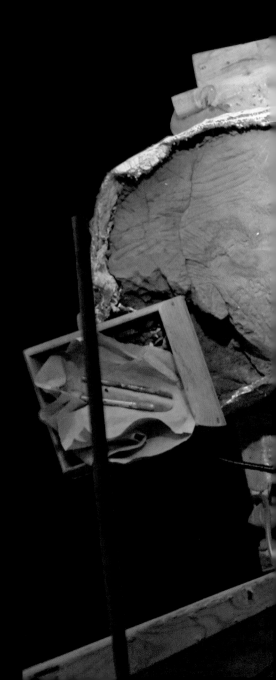

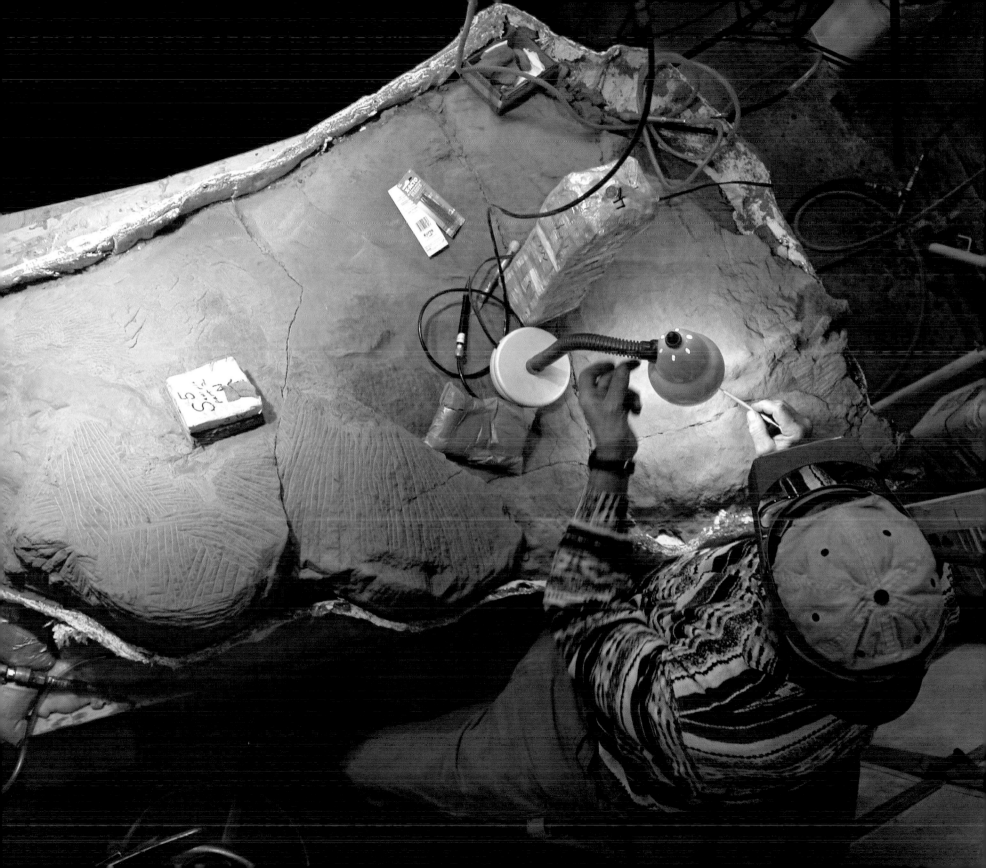

Tyler begins preparation work on one of Dakota's feet, which was carefully separated from the body block during the dig. The dinosaur's fossilized skin is almost the same color and texture as the surrounding rock, and Tyler needs great skill to make sure that he does not chip away any of Dakota's stony flesh. Helped by a strong light and a magnifying glass, he uses a dental pick to remove the matrix, grain by grain. It will take a team of preparators many, many months to finish the foot, but already skin scales are beginning to emerge.

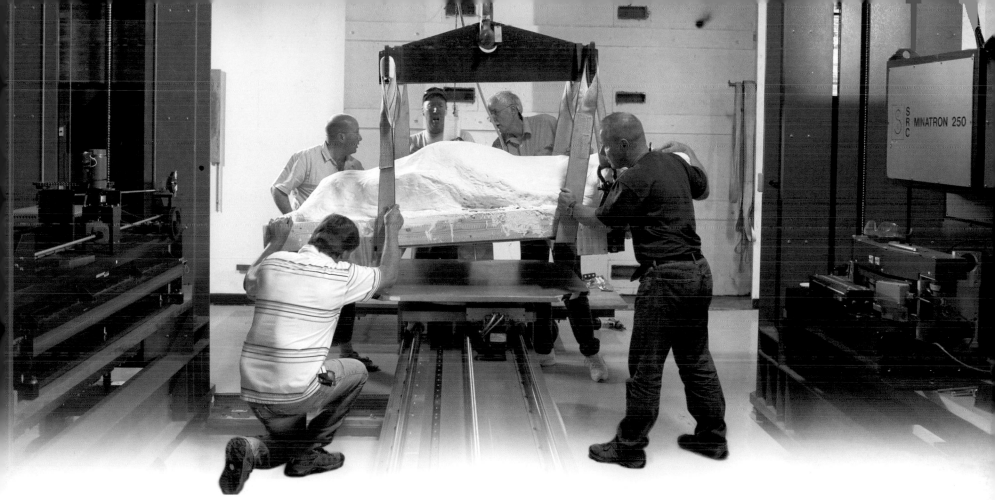

A few weeks later, Dakota is on the move again, plastered in a new field jacket to protect him during the journey. We're taking the dinosaur to California, to a scanning facility normally used to check space-shuttle parts for cracks. When we arrive, we carefully lower the dinosaur onto a sliding platform. The platform will move the block into the scanner, where x-ray beams will take a series of images from different angles.

When we scan the tail, we discover something pretty special—it *does* extend beyond the last vertebra. Tyler and I were right! Hadrosaur tails are longer than scientists previously thought! And this might be true of many other dinosaurs, so our discovery is very important for paleontology.

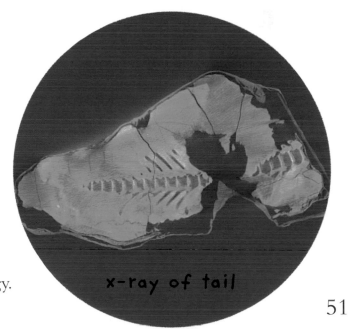

x-ray of tail

51

Back at our lab, prep work on the arm is finished. We have found something that has been seen only once before—a single fleshy pad on the palm. And, surprisingly, there are no hooflike fingernails. This confirms that hadrosaurs did not permanently walk on all fours—their hands were not tough enough for the job.

The foot that Tyler is preparing, however, does have hooves. Hadrosaur hooves were made of keratin, like your fingernails. Keratin is much tougher than skin, and Dakota's hooves are so well preserved that some of their keratin may not have turned to stone but survived! This is very, very rare and hugely exciting. It will tell us so much about what hadrosaurs are made of.

As we work on the body block, a few bones begin to emerge. This is strange—why isn't the chest area fully mummified?

body block

rib cage

shoulder blade

skin completely surrounds arm

hand

close-up of hand shows fleshy pad of palm

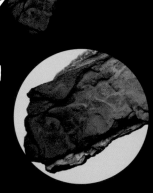

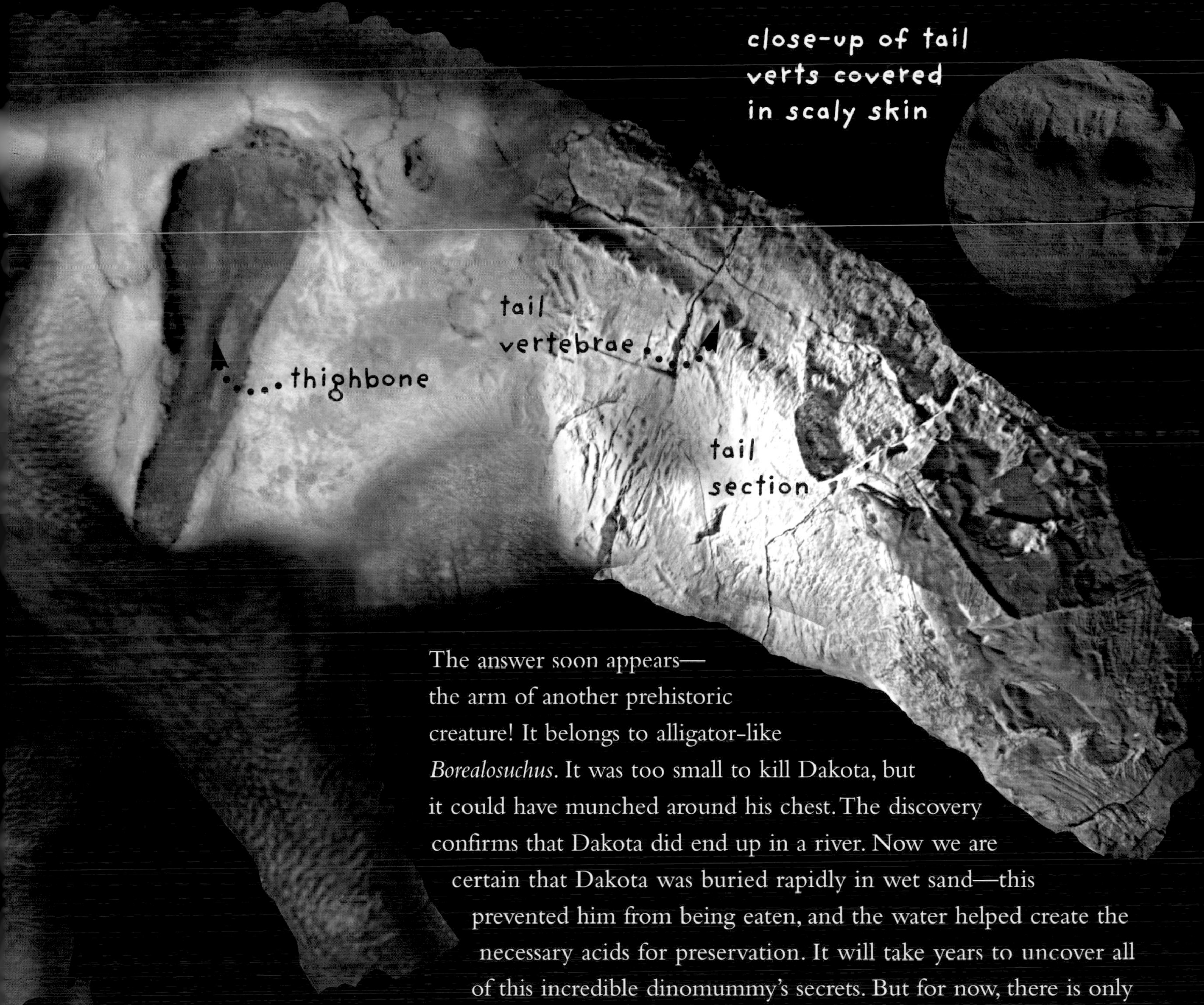

close-up of tail
verts covered
in scaly skin

tail
vertebrae . . . . .

. . . . . thighbone

tail
section

The answer soon appears—
the arm of another prehistoric
creature! It belongs to alligator-like
Borealosuchus. It was too small to kill Dakota, but
it could have munched around his chest. The discovery
confirms that Dakota did end up in a river. Now we are
certain that Dakota was buried rapidly in wet sand—this
prevented him from being eaten, and the water helped create the
necessary acids for preservation. It will take years to uncover all
of this incredible dinomummy's secrets. But for now, there is only
one likely explanation about how Dakota's life came to an end . . .

As night falls, Dakota's body lies in the muddy shallows of a river. His body is twisted and crumpled, battered by the river that delivered him there. Earlier, when the *T. rex* charged into the herd of hadrosaurs, Dakota fled in terror, and in his panic, he stumbled into the swollen river. Floodwaters were sweeping through Hell Creek, and they quickly knocked the dinosaur off his feet. The river washed away Dakota from the jaws of the *T. rex*, but they also overpowered him. Dakota drowned.

Now his body has come to rest in a bend of the river, where the current is gentle. A pack of scavenging *Borealosuchus* surrounds Dakota, and dark blood seeps out of him, staining the water. Dakota is sinking quickly into the wet sand, and soon only his chest will be exposed to the predators. In less than an hour, Dakota will slip out of sight.

Triassic

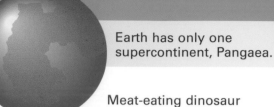

Earth has only one supercontinent, Pangaea.

Long-tailed pterosaur **Eudimorphodon** hunted fish.

Meat-eating dinosaur **Coelophysis** both hunted live prey and scavenged for dead animals.

Mammal-like reptile **Lystrosaurus** had two tusks.

Tiny **Lagosuchus** had legs similar to those of its later relatives, the dinosaurs.

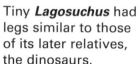

Mixosaurus, a marine reptile, not a dinosaur, had a long tail and paddlelike limbs.

Many scientists think that turkey-size predator **Eoraptor** was the world's first dinosaur!

Around 23 ft. long, **Plateosaurus** is the largest Triassic dinosaur ever discovered.

The age of the dinosaurs

The dinosaurs of the Hell Creek Formation lived 65 to 67 million years ago, at the end of the Cretaceous period. Dinosaurs have been around for 230 million years or so, developing and changing during the Triassic, Jurassic, and Cretaceous periods. Alongside the dinosaurs, giant reptiles swam in the oceans and soared through the skies.

56

Jurassic

Pangaea begins to break into separate continents.

Dimorphodon, a pterosaur, had a large, toothed beak.

Apatosaurus, a plant-eating giant, weighed around the same as four African elephants!

Lesothosaurus, from modern-day South Africa, could run quickly on two legs.

Megalosaurus was a powerful meat-eating predator.

Plant-eating **Stegosaurus** had two rows of plates along its back.

Dilophosaurus had two crests on its head that were probably used to attract mates.

Huayangosaurus, an older relative of *Stegosaurus*, was covered in protective spikes.

Plesiosaurus was a long-necked marine reptile.

Diplodocus was around the length of three double-decker buses!

144
million years ago

Earth's landmasses slowly
move to today's positions.

65
million years ago

Deinonychus had a
large, curved claw on
each foot for stabbing
or slashing its prey.

Small, feathered
Microraptor was
the only dinosaur
with four wings.

Quetzalcoatlus, with a wingspan
of up to 39 ft., was the largest
flying creature of all time.

Saltasaurus
belonged to the
same group of
dinosaurs as
Diplodocus and
Apatosaurus.

Muttaburrasaurus was a plant eater
found in many parts of
the world.

The stiff, bony tail of
Velociraptor helped this
clawed predator change
direction when running.

Spinosaurus had
a sail-like ridge, up
to 7 ft. high, which
may have helped it
scare away enemies.

Around the size of a small
elephant, plant-eating
Euoplocephalus had a tail club
and was heavily armored.

Carnivorous
Acrocanthosaurus
had a ridge down
its back because
of tall spines along
its backbone.

Bactrosaurus
was a hadrosaur
that lived in modern-
day east Asia.

Who's who in Hell Creek?

Many dinosaurs, reptiles, mammals, and birds lived in and alongside the rivers of Hell Creek. Some fed on the seeds and leaves of plants and trees; others preyed on smaller animals. If the dinosaurs of Hell Creek could speak, and if Tyler and I could go back in time to interview them, food would probably be a hot topic. Teeth and claws helped predators hunt, and armor plating and horns helped plant eaters avoid ending up on someone else's menu!

Ankylosaurus

What does your name mean?
"stiffened lizard"

How big are you?
Around 30 ft. long and 7 ft. high. I weigh a hefty 9,945 lbs.

Meat or vegetables?
Vegetables, please! I'm a herbivore.

Does anything eat you?
My armor plating puts off most predators, but occasionally I get hassled by desperate meat eaters.

You look a little weird.
Yes, I look like I'm suffering from a bad case of warts! It's the lumpy, bony plates in my skin. My head is very big, too. My skull is a big, bony block protecting my tiny brain.

Tell me something interesting.
I love clubbing in the Cretaceous! The bone at the tip of my tail has expanded into a club. Any predators who want a piece of me have to watch out for my bone-crushing tail blows!

Avisaurus

What does your name mean?
"bird lizard"

How big are you?
My wingspan is around 3 ft.

Meat or vegetables?
I eat meat, like one of your modern birds of prey. I hunt insects and small mammals, lizards, and birds.

Whose menu are you on?
I can fly away from most trouble, but if a large pterosaur is flying over Hell Creek, it might give me a hard time.

You look a little like a modern bird (yawn).
Wake up, please! Did you know that I have evolved from the meat-eating dinosaurs? And modern birds are my descendants. This means that the sparrows in your backyard are distant relatives of the dinosaurs!

Borealosuchus

What does your name mean?
"northern crocodile"
(more or less)

How big are you?
A little smaller than a modern croc—around 15 ft. long and 660 lbs. in weight.

Meat or vegetables?
I eat turtles, fish, and any mammals that are foolish enough to drink close to where I'm wallowing in a river.

Are you prey or a predator?
Weren't you listening? I'm a predator, of course! But I'm also a scavenger, which means that I eat dead animals.

What's interesting about you?
My family hasn't changed much in more than 100 million years—that's what's interesting about me! And that's because we survived when those wimpy dinosaurs died out!

Didelphodon

What does your name mean?
"opossum tooth"
(an opossum is a small mammal)

How big are you?
Around the size of a badger—20–39 in. long. And I weigh around 22–44 lbs.

Meat or vegetables?
Lizards, insects, bugs, and a few juicy plants, please.

Does anything eat you?
I'm too small for *T. rex* to spot, but unfortunately for me, *Saurornitholestes* has excellent eyesight . . .

Tell me something interesting.
I'm a marsupial, like a kangaroo. Yep, I raise my babies inside a pouch!

Edmontosaurus

What does your name mean?
"Edmonton lizard" (I was first found near Edmonton in Canada)

How big are you?
Very! Up to 39 ft. long, 10 ft. high, and 7,700 lbs. in weight.

Meat or vegetables?
Plants, please.

Prey or predator?
I prey on plants, but *T. rex* preys on me. Gulp!

Why do you look so strange? For a dinosaur, I don't look that weird, do I? I don't have strange spikes or horns. Perhaps my mouth looks a little odd to you. I am a hadrosaur, and we "duck-billed" dinosaurs have mouths shaped like beaks. Other members of the hadrosaur family look much weirder than me. They have strange head crests and inflatable nose pouches!

Eubaena

What does your name mean?
"good turtle"

How big are you?
I'm quite small really, around 12–20 in. long. I'm a lightweight 7-11 lbs.

Meat or vegetables?
I'll eat anything that will fit inside my mouth—fish, bugs, plants . . . I'm pretty adaptable, which is one of the reasons why I survived when the dinosaurs died out.

Does anything eat you?
Borealosuchus would like to crunch up my shell like a cracker if it got the chance . . .

You're just a turtle. What's interesting about you?
Don't you think it's interesting that turtles have lived for more than 200 million years? Humans haven't even been around for one million years!

Ornithomimus

What does your name mean?
"bird mimic" (I'm a little like a bird in some ways)

How big are you?
Around 15 ft. long, 8 ft. high, and 1,100 lbs. in weight.

Meat or vegetables?
Good question! I'm toothless, so I love soft fruit. But I never say no to a mouthful of mammal or lizard. I'm not fussy!

Does anything eat you?
Only if it can catch me! I'm possibly one of the fastest of all of the dinosaurs. My long legs help me run at speeds of around 30 mph.

You remind me of something . . .
Is it an ostrich? My body shape is similar to an ostrich's. Imagine me covered in feathers.

Tell me something interesting.
My bones are hollow, so I'm pretty light. This helps me run quickly.

Pachycephalosaurus

What does your name mean?
"thick-headed lizard" (don't laugh!)

How big are you?
Around 15 ft. long, 5 ft. high, and 2,200 lbs. in weight.

Meat or vegetables?
My teeth are excellent at shredding plants. They're not adapted for chewing meat.

Are you on anyone's menu?
I'm good at head butting. That usually keeps me out of trouble.

What's happening with your dome head?
The top of my skull is 10 in. thick—excellent for head butting my male buddies. This usually impresses the ladies!

Saurornitholestes

What does your name mean?
"lizard-bird thief"

How big are you?
Not very—around 6 ft. long and 3 ft. tall. I weigh around 88 lbs.

Meat or vegetables?
Just meat—any reptile or mammal will do.

Prey or predator?
I'm a predator and a superfast one—just look at the length of my legs!

You look a little like *Velociraptor*.
That's my cousin! We both have a long, curved claw on our second toe—perfect for ripping apart prey.

What's interesting about you?
I'm a bit of a mystery. You humans know very little about me. In Hell Creek, you've found only pieces of my skull.

Stegoceras

What does your name mean?
"roofed horn"

How big are you?
Around 7 ft. long, 3 ft. tall, and 110 lbs. in weight.

Meat or vegetables?
Plants, please. I'm a strict vegetarian.

Whose menu are you on?
As a small plant eater, I'm on quite a few of the meat eaters' menus, unfortunately.

You look like *Pachycephalosaurus*.
Good job! I'm a smaller relative. We both have thickened skulls for use as battering rams.

Tell me something interesting.
My neck vertebrae prevent my head from twisting when I am head butting.

Thescelosaurus

What does your name mean?
"marvelous lizard"

How big are you?
Around 13 ft. long, 3 ft. high, and only 220 lbs. in weight.

Meat or vegetables?
I'm a herbivore—so vegetables, please.

Prey or predator?
Prey, unfortunately . . .

You look a little boring. Why don't you have horns or armor plating? I don't need them because I don't stay around to fight. I'm a speed machine—I run away on my muscular, long legs.

Torosaurus

What does your name mean?
"pierced lizard" (the bone inside my head crest is pierced with holes)

How big are you?
Around 20 ft. long and 8 ft. high. At almost 16,500 lbs. in weight, I'm the heaviest resident of Hell Creek (my neck frill weighs a lot).

Meat or vegetables?
Vegetables, please, and lots of them. I need to eat a lot in order to provide energy for my large, bulky body.

Prey or predator?
Prey, if anyone can get past my 3-ft.-long horns.

You look a little like *Triceratops.*
We're related. We're both ceratopsians, which means that we have mouths like parrot beaks, and many of us have horns and neck frills.

Triceratops

What does your name mean?
"three-horned face"

How big are you?
Around 26 ft. long, 10 ft. high, and a hefty 13,200 lbs. in weight.

Meat or vegetables?
Vegetables. I'm a herbivore.

Prey or predator?
Alas, I'm prey, but with my weight and horns, I'm no brown-bag lunch!

Why do you look so weird?
My head is huge. And I have three long horns that I use to fight other *Triceratops* and to protect my family.

Tell me something interesting.
My neck frill is solid bone—my ceratopsian relatives have holes in theirs.

Tyrannosaurus rex

What does your name mean?
"tyrant-lizard king"—in other words, I'm the boss!

How big are you?
Enormous! 39 ft. long (some say longer), 13 ft. high, and 9,920 lbs. in weight.

Meat or vegetables?
Triceratops meat, *Edmontosaurus* meat, and any other meat that I can sink my teeth into. I don't bother with mammals—they're not even a mouthful.

Prey or predator?
What do you think? I am Hell Creek's top predator.

Why do you look so weird?
Maybe because my skull is almost 7 ft. long, with teeth the size of bananas. And I have tiny arms. But I wouldn't call me weird if I were you . . .

61

Glossary

acid a strong substance that can dissolve things

articulated arranged in the original position of the skeleton

badlands an area of wilderness with a dry climate, little vegetation, and soft ground that has been shaped by the wind and rain into hills

carnivore a meat eater

ceratopsian one of a group of plant-eating dinosaurs with beaked mouths. Some, such as *Triceratops*, had horns and a neck frill.

chemical a substance with specific characteristics

comet a ball of rock, dust, and ice, often with a "tail" of gas and dust, that circles the Sun

continent a large landmass on Earth

coyote a wild animal that is native to North America and is a relative of the wolf

digit a finger or a toe

dinomummy a dinosaur whose fossilized remains include some soft tissue, such as skin, as well as the skeleton

dinosaur a prehistoric reptile that lived between around 230 and 65 million years ago. *Dinosaur* means "terrible lizard."

evolve to change gradually

excavation the careful removal of a fossil from the ground and the recording of this process

extinction the dying out of a species or group of animals across the world

field jacket a layer of tinfoil covered in plaster-coated strips of sackcloth. It immobilizes and protects a dinosaur skeleton in the same way that a cast protects a broken limb.

fossil animal remains that have mineralized (turned to stone)

fossilization the slow change of an animal as it becomes a fossil over millions of years

frill the protective bony shield (part of the skull) that dinosaurs like *Triceratops* have

GPS receiver a Global Positioning System receiver calculates the exact position of its user with information sent by satellites

hadrosaur a medium-size plant-eating dinosaur with a mouth shaped like a duck's bill

Hell Creek Formation a layer of clay, mudstone, and sandstone that crosses the states of Montana, North Dakota, South Dakota, and Wyoming. The rock was deposited during the end of the Late Cretaceous period, burying dinosaurs of that age.

herbivore a plant eater

ice age a period when extensive ice sheets spread over parts of Earth

icthyosaur a marine reptile. *Ichthyosaur* means "fish lizard."

keratin — the tough material of which fingernails are made

lidar — light detection and range technology uses light to pinpoint a 3-D location

mammal — a warm-blooded, furry animal that produces milk to feed to its young

matrix — the rock immediately surrounding a dinosaur fossil

migration — the regular movement of a group of animals from one area to another to find food and water or to search for mates

mummified — the preserved state of the body of a person or animal caused by special conditions

overburden — the large quantity of rock and soil that needs to be dug away in order to access a fossil

paleontologist — a scientist who studies the history of all life on Earth

predator — an animal that hunts for food

prehistoric — relating to the time before humans lived

preparation — the careful removal of rock, using small tools, to reveal the bones or skin envelope of a dinosaur

preparator — someone who carries out preparation, or "prep," work

preservation — the condition of a specimen in terms of its decay or lack of decay. This is determined by how the animal died and was fossilized.

pterosaur — one of a group of flying reptiles. *Pterosaur* means "winged lizard."

raptor — a slang term for a small, carnivorous dinosaur that walks on two legs

reptile — a cold-blooded, furless animal. Many reptile species lay eggs.

scavenger — an animal that does not hunt for food, eating the remains of dead animals instead

scute — a bony plate, similar to those along a crocodile's back, that grows within the skin layer

siderite — a type of rock that is rich in iron

skin envelope — the outer layer of skin that encloses the skeleton and internal body parts

soft tissue — the parts of an animal that are not made of bone. Soft tissue includes muscle, skin, organs, and keratin.

species — a group of animals that share common physical characteristics

sulfur — a soft, pale yellow, nonmetallic substance

tsunami — a series of giant waves caused by earthquakes or volcanic eruptions

vertebra — a single bone that connects with other vertebrae to form the backbone (including the tail) of an animal

weathering out — the exposing of a fossil when the soil that covers it is worn away by harsh weather conditions such as heavy rain

x-ray — a form of radiation (energy that moves in waves) that can help produce a picture of the inside of an object

Index

Acknowledgments

The author wishes to thank: Tyler Lyson and the Marmarth Research Foundation and its team of volunteers; National Geographic Foundation (Research and Expedition) for grants that have supported the excavation, preparation, and science; Boeing Corporation for access to their CAT-scanning facility; Stephen Begin, who has sacrificed so much of his time and eyesight preparing Dakota; Black Hills Institute of Geological Research, South Dakota; Prof. Kent Stevens at the University of Oregon; my colleagues at the University of Manchester and The Manchester Museum. And many thanks especially to Jo, Alice, and Kate for allowing me vast quantities of time to explore a fascinating dinosaur called Dakota.

The publisher would like to thank: Tyler Lyson; Neal Larson, Pete Larson, Bob Farrar, and Larry Shaffer at the Black Hills Institute; Tony Cutting; Tim De Alwis; Simon Holland; Richard Platt

The publisher would like to thank the following for permission to reproduce their material. Every care has been taken to trace copyright holders. However, if there have been unintentional omissions or failure to trace copyright holders, we apologize and will, if informed, endeavor to make corrections in any future edition.

Key: *b* = bottom, *c* = center, *l* = left, *r* = right, *t* = top

Pages 1, 2–3, 4–5 Dean Steadman/Kingfisher Publications; 6 Phil Manning; 7 Dean Steadman/Kingfisher Publications; 8–9, 10–11, 12–13, 14–16, 16–17, 18–19, 20–21, 22–23, 24–25 Russell Gooday & Jon Hughes/Pixel Shack; 26–27, 28–29 Dean Steadman/Kingfisher Publications; 29*br* Pete Clayman; 30 Hannah Wilson; 31 Dean Steadman/Kingfisher Publications; 32–33 Dean Steadman/Kingfisher Publications (photographs); 32–33 Russell Gooday & Jon Hughes/Pixel Shack (digital artwork); 34 Dean Steadman/Kingfisher Publications & Tyler Lyson; 35 Tyler Lyson; 36–37, 38*r*–39 Dean Steadman/Kingfisher Publications; 38*l* Fritz Polking/Frank Lane Picture Agency; 40–41, 42 Dean Steadman/Kingfisher Publications; 43 National Geographic 2007; 44–45 National Geographic 2007; 46 Dean Steadman/Kingfisher Publications; 47 Russell Gooday & Jon Hughes/Pixel Shack; 48–49 Dean Steadman/Kingfisher Publications (with thanks to the Black Hills Institute for the skeleton); 50 Pete Clayman; 51 National Geographic 2007; 52*cl*, *cb* Tyler Lyson; 52–53, 53*tr* Black Hills Institute; 52–53 Russell Gooday & Jon Hughes/Pixel Shack (digital artwork); 54–55 Russell Gooday & Jon Hughes/Pixel Shack; 56–57 Steve Weston; 58*bl* Dean Steadman/Kingfisher Publications; 58–59 Russell Gooday & Jon Hughes/Pixel Shack except 58*br*, 59*tr* Steve Weston; 60–61 Russell Gooday & Jon Hughes/Pixel Shack except 60*tl*, 61*bl* Steve Weston; 62–63, 64 Dean Steadman/Kingfisher Publications